A KODANSHA COMICS TRADE PAPERBACK ORIGINAL

UQ HOLDER! VOLUME 17 COPYRIGHT © 2018 KEN AKAMATSU
ENGLISH TRANSLATION COPYRIGHT © 2019 KEN AKAMATSU

PUBLISHED IN THE UNITED STATES BY KODANSHA COMICS, AN IMPRINT OF KODANSHA USA PUBLISHING, LLC, NEW YORK.

PUBLICATION RIGHTS FOR THIS ENGLISH EDITION ARRANGED THROUGH KODANSHA LTD., TOKYO.

FIRST PUBLISHED IN JAPAN IN 2018 BY KODANSHA LTD., TOKYO.

ISBN 978-1-63236-802-7

PRINTED IN THE UNITED STATES OF AMERICA.

WWW.KODANSHACOMICS.COM

9 8 7 6 5 4 3 2 1

TRANSLATION: ALETHEA NIBLEY AND ATHENA NIBLEY
LETTERING: JAMES DASHIELL
EDITING: TIFF FERENTINI
KODANSHA COMICS EDITION COVER DESIGN: PHIL BALSMAN

CAN A FARMER SAVE THE WORLD? FIND OUT IN THIS FANTASY MANGA FOR FANS OF *SWORD ART ONLINE* AND *THAT TIME I GOT REINCARNATED AS A SLIME!*

I'M STANDING ON A MILLION LIVES

By
Akinari Nao

Original Story by
Naoki Yamakawa

Yusuke Yotsuya doesn't care about getting into high school—he just wants to get back home to his game and away from other people. But when he suddenly finds himself in a real-life fantasy game alongside his two gorgeous classmates, he discovers a new world of possibility and excitement. Despite a rough start, Yusuke and his friend fight to level up and clear the challenges set before them by a mysterious figure from the future, but before long, they find that they're not just battling for their own lives, but for the lives of millions...

KODANSHA
COMICS

UQ HOLDER!

STAFF

Ken Akamatsu
Takashi Takemoto
Kenichi Nakamura
Keiichi Yamashita
Yuri Sasaki
Madoka Akanuma

Thanks to Ran Ayanaga

CREAK

TO BE CONTINUED IN VOLUME 18!

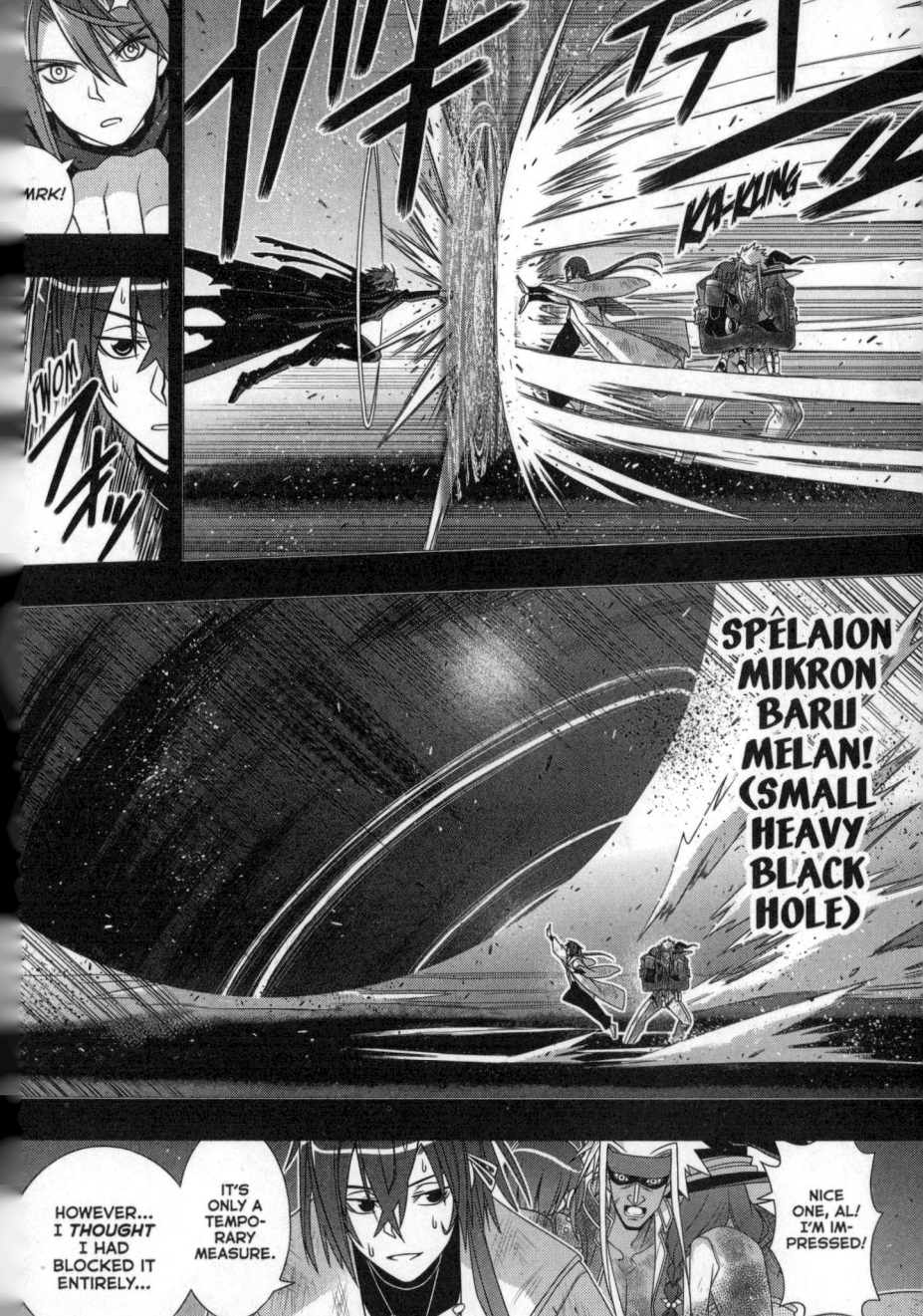

THAT'S...! THAT'S ONE OF IALDA'S TECHNIQUES! IT WILL LATCH ON TO THEIR SOULS, EATING AWAY AT THEM UNTIL IT FUSES WITH THEM, MAKING THEM HER PUPPETS.

HNGH ...

AH ...

WAIT, RAKAN!

WAIT FOR ME, LADIES!!

HNGH!

FWRAAM

I'M~!

NODOKA-SAN! YUE-SAN!

2025
THE
ASTEROID BELT

MAGICAL WORLD
AGARTHA ASTEROID
NAGI IALDA'S BASE OF OPERATIONS

MAYBE THIS IS A GOOD PLACE TO LAY OUT THE DIFFERENCES BETWEEN THESE TWO WORLDS.

HUH ...?

THE EFFECTS OF ASUNA KAGURAZAKA'S ABSENCE DIDN'T END THERE.

THEN WE HAVE THIS WORLD— THE WORLD WITH NO ASUNA KAGURAZAKA.

2004

WE'LL CALL IT WORLD A.

HA HA HA

GRR ...!

2066

TO BE CONTINUED...

FIRST, WE HAVE THE OTHER WORLD— THE ONE WITH ASUNA KAGURA-ZAKA.

2004

WE'LL CALL THIS WORLD A' (A PRIME).

2011

HAPPY END!

WOULD BUILD UP A RELATIONSHIP OF TRUST WITH THE BOY NEGI, THOUGH IN A COMPLETELY DIFFERENT FORM.

AND THE TWO GIRLS, WHO HAD THEIR HEARTS BROKEN SO QUICKLY AND CLEANLY IN THE OTHER WORLD,

THE MEMORY OF THE GIRL WHO WAS NO LONGER WITH THEM...

...WOULD GROW TO TAKE UP AN EVEN BIGGER PLACE IN HIS MIND AND HEART.

...MAKING THEIR RELATIONSHIPS SOMEWHAT MORE COMPLICATED.

ALL OF THESE FACTORS WOULD AFFECT HIS ADOLESCENCE AND THE ROMANTIC PATTERNS OF THE GIRLS SURROUNDING HIM...

NODOKA-SAN, YUE-SAN!

TODAY...WAS GRADUATION DAY.

THAT'S RIGHT.

NEGI-SENSEI!

WE, UM...WE TALKED IT OVER, AND DECIDED...

WHAT...?

BUT...UM, WE'RE NOT HERE TO GET THE RESPONSES WE ASKED FOR.

Y-YES!

YES?!

...IS THE STORY OF A WORLD WITHOUT ASUNA.

SHH

STAGE 148: WHERE THE PATH OF DESTINY DIVERGES

UM... ER... RIGHT...

UH... UMMM...

ER... UM... WELL... THAT IS.

UH... UM... SE-SENSEI...

YUP. WE PICKED IT OUT TOGETHER.

DOES HE HAVE A NAME?

ZERO ...

I SEE... SO THIS IS YOUR REASON.

KA-CHAK

WHAAA? WHY NOT? I SEE NO REASON TO TURN HIM DOWN!

I WILL NOT!!

STOP MAKING EXCUSES AND GO ACCEPT HIS PROPOSAL!

KEEPING YOUR OPTIONS OPEN, EH?! GYA HA HA HA! THAT'S AN EVIL WITCH FOR YOU! YOU LIKE HIM! YOU LOVE HIM!

IT'S NOT WHAT IT LOOKS LIKE!

WHOOOAA?! YOU TURN DOWN HIS PROPOSAL THEN KISS HIM?! YOU LITTLE SO-AND-SO!!

I'M NOT IN LOVE WITH HIM! THERE'S NOTHING ROMANTIC BETWEEN US!

I WILL NOT!

POKE POKE POKE POKE POKE

IT'S BEEN LONG ENOUGH! GO MAKE YOURSELF HAPPY, MISTRESS!

UGH, JUST SHUT UP, YOU PIECE OF JUNK!

NOOGIE NOOGIE NOOGIE NOOGIE NOOGIE NOOGIE!!

HMMM?

HMMM-MMM-MM?!

HOW DO YOU REALLY FEEL?!

THERE YOU GO AGAIN AND AGAIN AND AGAIN! THIS IS ME YOU'RE TALKING TO! QUIT IT WITH THE BOLD FRONT AND JUST BE YOURSELF!

SIGH...

パタン (SHUT)

YOU GET OUT OF HERE, TOO!

ARE YOU SURE ABOUT THIS?

OOHH オオオオ

ZERO...

オオオオ OOO

HH オオオ

Z-S-H-H DY'

!

...SIGH.

FIRST, I NEED TO BE READY...

YOU'RE READY NOW, AND YOU'RE STRONG ENOUGH TO TAKE IT.

YOU HAVE THE RIGHT TO KNOW ALL THE ANSWERS.

YOU'RE RIGHT, TŌTA.

...

EVERYTHING I KNOW, ANYWAY.

ALL RIGHT. I'LL TELL YOU EVERYTHING.

HM?

?

IT WILL ONLY TAKE FIVE MINUTES.

BUT BEFORE THAT, COULD YOU GIVE ME SOME TIME ALONE WITH HER?

...!

BUT FIRST, I WOULD LIKE TO...

OH, RIGHT. SURE, YUKIHIME.

OF COURSE.

I...I THINK IT WILL MAKE MORE SENSE IF YOU SEE CHACHAZERO'S MEMORIES FIRST.

ほう！

M...
IS...
TRESS.

M...
IS...
TRESS.

ZERO...

CHA-CHA...

...!

...SHE USED TO BE YOUR PARTNER.

I HEARD THAT...

YUKI-HIME...

SFF

WHICH MEANS THEY'D BEEN FRIENDS FOR 700 YEARS...

WHEN I MET PAST YUKIHIME, SHE HAD THAT DOLL WITH HER THEN, TOO.

YES.

YUKI-HIME...

...ISN'T...

...ME.

THAT...

YES. FROM THIS GUY.

BUT WE WERE *SUPPOSED* TO HEAR ABOUT *OUR* WORLD, NOT THAT OTHER ONE.

ANYWAY, WE GOT INTERRUPTED BY THAT TERRORIST ATTACK.

CLUNK

I HAD INTENDED TO SHOW THEM HER MEMORIES.

EVEN WITH ASUNA KAGURA-ZAKA'S POWER...

...IT SHOULDN'T BE POSSIBLE TO SAVE NAGI!!

THAT CAN'T BE TRUE!

ガシャ CLANK

I SUSPECT... SOME KIND OF MIRACLE OCCURRED.

...

...ALL THE WAY TO ITS RIDICULOUS END, THEN MAYBE...

WAIT...NO. IF I HAD KEPT FOLLOWING THE SAME PATH AS THOSE BOUNDLESSLY OPTIMISTIC IDIOTS...

...NO.

THAT'S... NOT POSSIBLE.

BUT ME? LIVING HAPPILY EVER AFTER WITH NAGI?

OR OUR FRIEND IALDA HAD A CHANGE OF HEART RIGHT BEFORE THEY DESTROYED HER, AND DECIDED TO LET HER HOST LIVE...

NO... THAT WOULDN'T HAPPEN.

...

A... MIR... ACLE?

HMM, NOT SATISFIED, EH? IT'S TRUE, YOU COULD DO WITH SOME MORE PADDING.

WHAT? YOU DIDN'T LIKE THAT? YOU'RE SO HIGH MAINTENANCE.

W...WAIT. PLEASE, NOT SO DIRECT.

NEVER MIND THAT!!

BAM

WOULD YOU STOP THAT?!

YEEEE-ARRGH?!

YES, BEAUTIFUL.

IT'S IMPORTANT TO KEEP THINGS BALANCED. THERE. BUTTOCKS, BREASTS, BELLY, THIGHS, UPPER ARMS.

POOF

POOF

POOF

POOF

UH... UHHHHH?

OH.

RIGHT.

BAM

BAM

THIS ISN'T GETTING US ANY-WHERE!!

WE'RE HERE TO REPORT!!

REPORT?

WHA–

ZHOOM

ARE YOU SURE ABOUT THIS, EVANGELINE?

?!

DANA ANANGA JAGAN-NATHA!!

YOU'RE STILL HERE ?!

HO HO HO HO.

Y-YOU !!

DUN

DUN

BUT ARE YOU SURE ABOUT THIS?

... HIM.

WHAT LINE?

YOU STAY OUT OF THIS, INCOMPETENT!!

AND BESIDES, YOU DON'T SEEM TO UNDERSTAND, YUKIHIME, BUT I HAVE SOME THINGS I'D LIKE TO SAY TO YOU ABOUT THE WAY YOU EDUCATED HIM THOSE TWO YEARS!

? WHAT ARE YOU TALKING ABOUT?

WHAT LINE WOULD I EVER CROSS WITH MR. GRADE-SCHOOL BRAIN?!

KURŌMARU WOULD DEFINITELY BE BETTER OFF—

WHY SHOULD I CARE? IN FACT, PERSONALLY, I WOULD ENDORSE KURŌMARU.

KURŌMARU? ?

OR KURŌMARU.

LIKE THOSE LITTLE GIRLS.

IF YOU ACT TOO INDIFFERENT, SOMEONE MIGHT TAKE HIM FROM YOU.

MAYBE *I'LL* TAKE HIM.

ALL RIGHT, THEN.

Y-Y-Y-YUKIHIME IS STILL HIS TOP CHOICE!! WH-WH-WH-WHAT IF SHE DID?! NO, REALLY, AS LONG AS I CAN BE WITH HIM, I REALLY DON'T CARE WHAT HE WANTS TO DO, PERSONALLY. I REALLY DON'T. B-B-B-B-BUT IF YUKIHIME GOT SERIOUS ABOUT HIM, THERE'S NO TELLING WHAT COULD HAPPEN. I M-M-M-MIGHT BE IN TROUBLE!

ABUH-BUH-BUH-BWUH

I-I-I-IT'S NOT LIKE THAT WITH ME AND HIM ANYWAY!

I W-W-W-W-W-WOULDN'T CARE IF YOU DID!

WHA—

HRRGH ...

AH HA HA HA HA! AND I WAS AFRAID YOU'D NEVER GROW OUT OF THAT GRADE-SCHOOL MENTALITY!

WHAT'S THAT SUPPOSED TO MEAN ?!

HA HA HA HA! OF COURSE, *THAT'S* WHY YOUR FACE IS SO RED. YOU'RE FINALLY BECOMING AWARE OF YOUR SEXUALITY.

BAM

SHH フ キ フ S H H

...

ボ T BOING

JIGGLE フ リ リ JIGGLE

MAYBE I SHOULD START RE-SEARCH-ING TRANS-FORMA-TION MAGIC, TOO. COULD TAKE YEARS, THOUGH.

HMMMMMM. SO IT REALLY IS ABOUT THE BOING FACTOR. THAT'S IT, ISN'T IT? ALL THAT JIGGLING?

HM? YOU WANT TO SEE MORE? I DON'T MIND.

JIGGLE フルン

HEY! SHOULD YOU REALLY BE DOING THIS TO SOMEONE YOU SUPPOSEDLY DUMPED?!

I'M PRETTY SURE YOU SHOULDN'T !!

STAGE 147: MEMORY

CHATTER CHATTER
TEP TEP TEP TEP TEP

THAT'S THE ONLY WAY TO...

DON'T EVER STOP THINKING ABOUT IT.

THINK ABOUT IT, TŌTA-KUN.

GOOD. THAT'S GOOD ENOUGH.

AHH?! AFTER THAT EMBARRASSING NOT-GOODBYE? YOU'RE NEVER GONNA LOOK COOL, STUPID!

JINBEI-SAN! I'M TRYING TO GIVE A COOL SEMPAI SPEECH HERE!

YOU'RE DRUNK, AREN'T YOU?

LOOK AT YOU, A COUPLE OF DUDES GAZING AT THE NIGHT SEA TOGETHER!

KA-FWAM

WAA-AH HA HA HA!

GU-HACK?!

EW! GROSS!

BU-BWAGH!

PFFT

GER-BWUGH?!

GLUG GLUG GLUG

CHUG! CHUG!

GO ON, HAVE A DRINK!!

YOU BETTER HIT THIS BACK TO ME! 'CAUSE IF YOU DON'T, YOU'RE DEAD!

THIS IS NOT FUN! WHY ARE YOU TAKING A FIGHTING STANCE?!

THIS IS GONNA BE FUN, GENGORŌ! STAND RIGHT THERE!

OH, RIGHT! 'CAUSE YOU DON'T HAVE ANY EXTRA LIVES NOW!

WHOA! NEVER SEEN YOU FREAK OUT LIKE THAT BEFORE.

WHAT ARE YOU DOING, MASTER?! WHAT IF I DIED OF ACUTE ALCOHOL POISONING?!

YOU ARE DEFINITELY DRUNK!

AME AMEHA!

KABLOOEY

HAAHH

RAR

RAR

GENGORŌ-SEMPAI!

BUT THAT WOULD BE A MISTAKE.

DON'T YOU AGREE?

...YEAH.

AND SO, TŌTA-KUN...

HEH...

...

CHEERS! ♪

LET'S TOAST! CHEERS, CHEERS! ♪

NICE WORK TO YOU, TOO, LADIES!

ALLLLL RIGHT! NOW IT'S TIME TO CELEBRATE!

MAN, WHAT RELIEF.

HA HA HA.

ALL THAT DRAMA OVER NOTHING.

OVER THERE.

WHERE'S TŌTA?

WA HA HA HA

OH...

CUTLASS.

SO... YOUR SISTER.

!

I'M SO SORRY ABOUT WHAT HAPPENED !!

...

HM? WHAT IS IT, TŌTA-KUN?

UH... GENGORŌ SEMPAI.

OH, UMM.

I JUST ...

HE SURVIVED! AND HE'S FIT AS A FIDDLE!

DU-DUN

HA HA HA HA HA

WA HA HA HA HA! WELL, THERE YOU HAVE IT!

BAM

BAM

I ♥ MIHASHIRA

HA HA HA HA.

HA...

GLARE... IS SOMETHING FUNNY, TŌTA KONOE?

THAT'S NOT WHY I...

NO!

FLINCH

DON'T LAUGH SO HARD, JINBEI-SAN.

MAN, AND AFTER THAT HEROIC GOODBYE AND EVERYTHING. HA HA HA HA!

SO I PICKED HIM UP BEFORE HE HIT THE GROUND.

SEE, HE GETS A NEW LIFE WHEN HE DOES A GOOD DEED! AND IF SAVING TEN THOUSAND PEOPLE ISN'T A GOOD DEED, I DON'T KNOW WHAT IS!

SMACK

SMACK

GAAAAPE

CHATTER

CHATTER

NII-CHAN...

Z-ISHH

NO, HE TOLD ME TO KEEP QUIET AS LONG AS POSSIBLE. HE'S TOO EMBARRASSED.

TŌTA-KUN?

YEAH. YUP, THAT'S RIGHT.

HUH?

WAH HA HA HA

... ...

...

Z-ZSHH
Aｰｰｰ..

NGH ...

Z-ZSHH

NO...

IT IS. IT'S ALL... MY...

THIS ISN'T YOUR FAULT.

... TŌTA.

SFF

CLENCH...

GEN-GORŌ-SEM-PAA-AAI!!

S... SEM- PAI!

GEN- GORŌ- SEMPAI!

NII- CHAN!

!

GENGO...

GRR...

...

YES, SIR.

WHAT DO YOU SAY?

...

THIS IS GOOD-BYE.

THEN ...

ゴ゛ザ ザ゛ WHOOOOSH ザ ザ゛

SEM-PAI!

S...

SEMPAI!

YEAH.

WHEN I GET TO THE OTHER SIDE, I'LL TELL YOU AS MANY AS YOU WANT.

BE READY FOR ME.

KRRR

KRIK

I'M STILL AGAINST IT.

BUT GENGORŌ-SEMPAI... YOU WERE AGAINST THIS PLAN.

B... BUT...

SO YOU...

WHOOOSH

...UNTIL YOU FIND THE ANSWER.

...ARE GOING TO HAVE TO KEEP WALKING...

...

SO DON'T LET IT BOTHER YOU. UNDER-STAND?

I'VE ALREADY SPENT CLOSE TO 30 YEARS ON THIS SIDE.

I WAS BASICALLY READY TO DIE ANY TIME.

...

BUT...

SEMPAI...

...

MASTER.

YOU NEVER DID ACKNOWLEDGE ME AS YOUR APPRENTICE ...

...IS THAT I HAVEN'T HEARD EVEN ONE HUNDREDTH OF THE TALES OF YOUR HEROICS.

MY ONE REGRET ...

BUT I'M GOING ON AHEAD.

AND WE PULLED IT OFF WITH ZERO CASUALTIES... TŌTA.

THIS CASE IS CLOSED.

I... I...

GENGORŌ-SEMPAI... YOU MEAN...

G...

WITHOUT ANY EXTRA LIVES, I'M GOING TO BURN UP WHEN I ENTER EARTH'S ATMOSPHERE.

My seconds of invincibility are up, too.

I JUST... HADN'T THOUGHT ABOUT THE NEXT STEP.

S... SEMPAI...

IT'S ALL RIGHT, TŌTA-KUN.

THAT'S WHY I WANTED TO TALK TO YOU.

I KNEW YOU WERE GOING TO BE BROKEN UP ABOUT THIS.

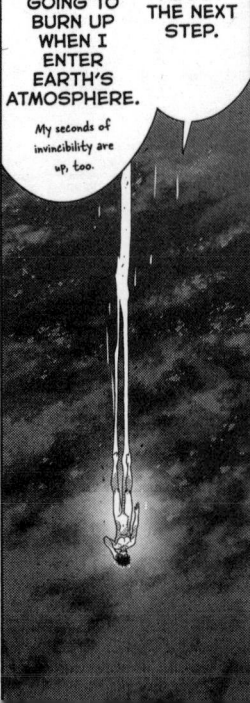

WELL...

UH...

OH GOOD! YOU'RE OKAY!

YOU, TOO... BUT KIRIË, WHAT ABOUT GENGORŌ-SEMPAI?!

KIRIË?!

TŌTA! RE-SPOND!

GENGORŌ-SEMPAI!!

TŌTA-KUN?

...KUN.

I CAN TALK TO YOU ONE LAST TIME.

GOOD.

WHERE? WELL...

I'D SAY I'M CURRENTLY FALLING DOWN TO YOU.

WHERE ARE YOU NOW?!

I MEAN MY IM-MORTALITY DOESN'T ALLOW FOR THE SAME KIND OF RECK-LESS-NESS YOURS DOES.

WH-WHAT DO YOU MEAN?!

WHAT... LAST TIME?

I'LL GIVE YOU EVERYTHING I HAVE LEFT, TERRORISTS!!

RELEASE ALL REMAINING LIVES!!

TICK

=000

BOOM

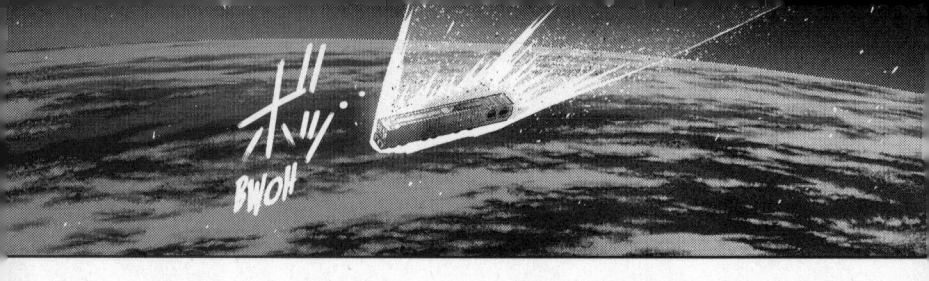

BWOH

ARE MY BARRIERS FACING THE RIGHT WAY?!

NO! I CAN'T SEE THE TARGET ANYMORE!!

ALL I CAN DO IS TRUST MY INSTINCTS!!

RRAAHH!

=057

AT THIS RATE...

BOOM

ADDITIONAL RELEASE X50!!

ONE OF ME DOESN'T EVEN LAST FIVE SECONDS!

POW POW

=160

POW—

POW POW

=183

POW

HNGH!

HRRGH...

X35

ADDITIONAL RELEASE!

BWOH

POW

URRGH!

RRAAHH!

GEN-GORŌ-SEMPAI!

NII-CHAN, WE'RE FALLING!

TŌTA, BRACE FOR EENTRY!

!!

GEN-GORŌ-SEMPAI!

BOOM

DEPLOY MAGIC CIRCLES !!

VWOMM

THE HEAT RAYS FROM THE BLAST CAN KILL ONE OF ME INSTANTLY, BUT I'LL HAVE THREE SECONDS OF INVINCIBILITY AFTER I RESPAWN.

BOOM

...AND SOFTEN THE EXPLOSION THROUGH MAGICAL INTERFERENCE!!

I'LL USE THAT IMPOSSIBLE MOMENT TO CONJURE BARRIERS...

WHOOSH

STOCKED LIVES SIMULTA- NEOUS RELEASE X29!

BAH

BEEP

00:00.00

NOT SURPRISINGLY, I ONLY MANAGED TO GET ONE KILOMETER AWAY.

FROM THIS POSITION, IT'S SURE TO DO ENORMOUS DAMAGE TO THE STATION.

I'LL JUST HAVE TO DISPOSE OF IT MYSELF.

00:14:20

HEY, YOU GONNA BE OKAY, GENGORŌ?

00:08.27

I SUPPOSE IT'S TIME TO GIVE IN TO THE INEVITABLE.

EIGHT SECONDS LEFT.

I ONLY HAVE ONE SECOND. HERE GOES.

HEY, GENGORŌ...

THEN WOULD YOU KINDLY SHUT UP? I NEED A FAIR AMOUNT OF CONCENTRATION FOR THIS.

NO, WHY WOULD YOU SAY THAT?

OH, ARE YOU ACKNOWLEDGING ME AS YOUR APPRENTICE?

"WHO CAN SAY?" IS THAT ANY WAY TO TALK TO YOUR MASTER?

WHO CAN SAY?

IF I'M GOING TO HAVE TO GO OUT INTO SPACE, I'D LIKE TO WEAR A SPACE-SUIT.

AND I'M NOT AS CONFIDENT IN MY IM-MORTALITY AS ALL OF YOU.

THAT'S TRUE.

B-BUT GENGORŌ-SEMPAI!!! YOU'RE ALL ALONE BACK THERE!

EVERYTHING YOU CAN DO...MEANS USING UP YOUR LIVES TO...

HEY, GENGORŌ, ARE YOU SURE ABOUT THIS?

IF I WERE MARIO, IT WOULD BE MORE THAN ENOUGH TO BEAT THE GAME.

NO, COME ON.

IS...IS THAT A LOT? OR NOT VERY MUCH?

FORTUNATELY, I HAVE 217 LIVES LEFT.

DON'T BE RIDICULOUS! DO YOU HAVE ANY IDEA HOW FAR AWAY HE IS? BESIDES, THAT WAS MY LAST SPARE!

WHA –!

I CAN USE A LIGHTNING-SPEED SHUNDŌ GET TO GENGORŌ-SEMPAI AND...

KARIN-SEMPAI! USE THE LIGHTNING CYLINDER ON ME!

IF IT WAS THAT WOMAN'S IDEA, THEN IT MAY BE THAT THEY WANTED YOU TO TASTE DEFEAT IN WHATEVER FORM IT HAD TO TAKE.

THOSE... BASTARDS. THEY WOULD...

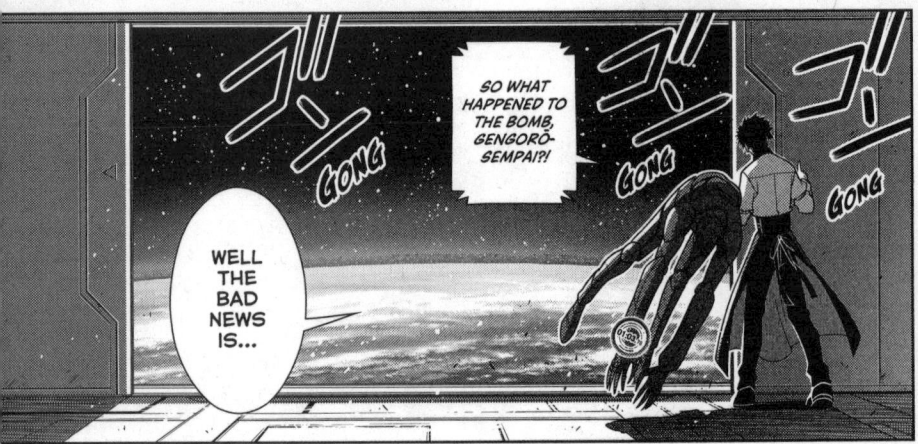

SO WHAT HAPPENED TO THE BOMB, GENGORŌ-SEMPAI?!

GONG GONG GONG

WELL THE BAD NEWS IS...

AND THAT'S WHEN THE BOMB'S TIMER SPED UP.

ONCE THE BOMB WAS DISCOVERED, THE STATION'S BOMB DISPOSAL GOT TO WORK, BUT I CUT OFF THE CYBORG'S HEAD FOR QUESTIONING.

WE ONLY HAVE 57 SECONDS UNTIL IT GOES OFF.

00:57.21

WHAT ...?!

I'LL DO EVERYTHING I CAN.

DON'T PANIC.

S-SO WHAT'S GONNA HAPPEN TO THE STATION?

THERE WAS ANOTHER BOMB HERE IN THE STATION.

AND THIS ONE IS REAL.

IT'S INSIDE THE TERRORIST'S STOMACH.

YES. BUT SEVERAL TIMES SMALLER THAN THE ONE FROM THE FIRST WAVE.

ANOTHER NUCLEAR BOMB?!

WHAT...?

IT TURNS OUT WE WERE RIGHT TO CAPTURE HIM ALIVE. WE WERE VERY CLOSE TO THE STATION.

AND IT WAS SET UP TO EXPLODE IMMEDIATELY IF HE HAD BEEN KILLED.

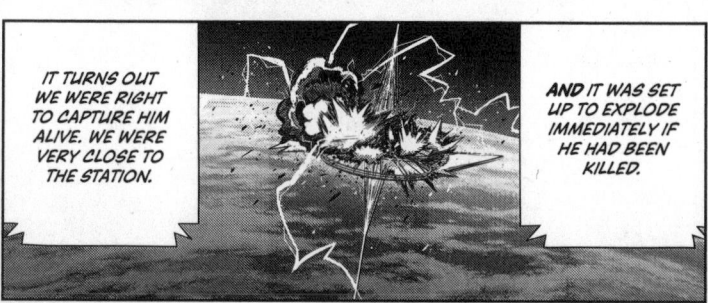

WHA...

YOU... YOU MEAN...

THIS BOMB IS JUST A REALISTIC FAKE!!

BUT IT'S EMPTY!

HE'S RIGHT, NII-CHAN! I DIDN'T CHECK ON THE INSIDE BEFORE!

YOU MUST HAVE NOTICED SOMETHING WASN'T RIGHT, TŌTA KONOE.

WE MEAN IT WAS A DECOY. IT'S A TRAP WITHIN A TRAP.

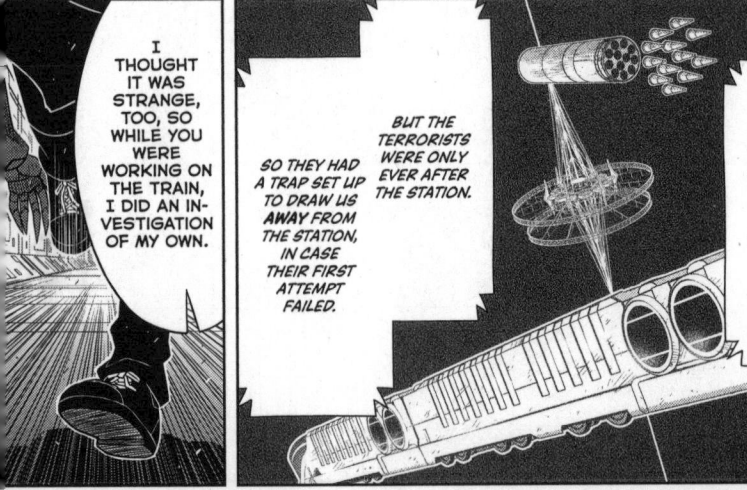

I THOUGHT IT WAS STRANGE, TOO, SO WHILE YOU WERE WORKING ON THE TRAIN, I DID AN IN-VESTIGATION OF MY OWN.

SO THEY HAD A TRAP SET UP TO DRAW US *AWAY* FROM THE STATION, IN CASE THEIR FIRST ATTEMPT FAILED.

BUT THE TERRORISTS WERE ONLY EVER AFTER THE STATION.

THERE SHOULD HAVE BEEN *TWO* NUCLEAR BLASTS LAST TIME—ONE AT THE STATION AND ONE ON LAND.

THE TRAIN WAS HEADED FOR EARTH WHETHER OR NOT KIRIÉ TURNED BACK TIME.

...?

...

IT'S...NOT EXPLODING?

FSHH...
シラウウ..

HUH ...?

HUH ?

G...GEN-GORŌ-SEMPAI?

IT LOOKS LIKE THAT NUCLEAR BOMB IS A DUMMY.

NO, TŌTA KONOE.

IS... IS IT A DUD...?

IM-POS-SIBLE ...

WELL, THAT'S SIMPLE. WE'LL JUST MOVE THE WHOLE TRAIN CAR TO BUY SOME TIME BEFORE IT EXPLODES!

THE DETONATOR IS THE LATEST IN MECHANICAL-MAGIC HYBRIDS.

IT WON'T LET US DESTROY THE BOMB DIRECTLY THROUGH PHYSICAL MEANS, OR TAMPER WITH IT USING TELEPORTATION MAGIC OR ANYTHING LIKE THAT.

MAXIMUM TELEKINESIS !!

LIGHTNING SPEED SHUNDŌ!!

SO WE HAVE ONE SECOND BEFORE IT FIGURES US OUT?!

YES! AND WITH TIME TO SPARE.

I WOULDN'T EXACTLY SAY THREE MINUTES IS TIME TO SPARE...

OKAY!! WE MOVED ALL THE PASSENGERS FROM CAR 9 INTO THE NEXT CAR!

LET'S DO THIS!!

ALL RIGHT !!

IT'S OKAY. THERE ARE NO DEFECTS IN THIS PLAN...I THINK.

NOW...I CAN PUT AN END TO HER EVIL.

SHINMEI SCHOOL SECRET TECH-NIQUE...

YES, SIR!!

TAKE IT AWAY, KURŌMARU!!

RIGHT!

YEAH!

NOW GET TO IT!!

OKAY.

...

TIME LEFT TO STOP THE BOMB: 54 MINUTES

SHOULD WE HAVE A SPECIALIST MAKE SURE WE KNOW HOW THE DETONATOR WORKS?

I THINK IT COULD WORK, TŌTA-KUN.

IT'S DEFINITELY RECKLESS...

WHAT DO YOU THINK?

THIS PLAN WILL NEED SOMEONE TO BLOCK THE SHOCK WAVES AND RADIATION FROM THE EXPLOSION.

I'M GOING WITH YOU.

KARIN-SEMPAI?

WAIT A MINUTE, TŌTA.

WHAT?

OH.

HEH...

THANKS, SEMPAI.

...! GOOD POINT. OKAY.

THIS'LL BE A PIECE OF CAKE.

BUT WE'RE A WHOLE TEAM OF IMMORTAL SUPER-HUMANS.

HEH HEH... I WAS JUST THINKING.

MAYBE I CAN'T DO IT ON MY OWN.

I FOUND THE BOMB AND FIGURED OUT HOW THE DETONATOR WORKS!!

ZAN

NII-CHAN! I JUST SEARCHED ALL THE TRAIN CARS!!

TŌTA KONOE!!

UH!

YEAH!

NICE WORK! LET'S TURN THIS OVER TO YUKIHIME AND GET A SPECIALIST TO CONFIRM!

WELL DONE!

ONLY A SPIRIT LIKE SANTA-KUN COULD HAVE FINISHED THE SEARCH SO QUICKLY.

OKAY!

WHAT? Y-YOU DID? THAT'S MY SANTA!!

IT'S IN A FREIGHT CONTAINER IN THE CARGO HOLD ON CAR 9!

THAT LITTLE...

...

YOU CAN'T FIX THIS ONE.

!

TŌTA.

SO? DO YOU HAVE A PLAN?

NO, IT'S OKAY!

YEAH!!

SFX: PA-... / KING

HUH ....?

AFTER ALL YOUR BIG TALK, I ASSUME YOU HAVE SOME KIND OF PLAN?!

FORGET ABOUT WHO STARTED THIS— THE IMPORTANT THING IS TO STOP IT!

...TŌTA!

TŌTA KONOE!

!!

ZSHH WHHHAA....

GOTTY
CLUNK

YUKI-HIME.

Y...

STAGE 146: ROLL OUT THE EXTRA LIVES

WHHAAA
ZSHH...

TŌTA...

I'M SORRY ABOUT YOUR SISTER.

THERE WERE JUST TOO MANY UNKNOWN VARIABLES TO JUSTIFY LETTING HER GO.

NO, THAT'S ...

NO...

WHAM

WHA...

... YOU. ... DARE

HOW ...

SNAP
KRIK
KRIK
KRIK

NII-SAN... THA[T] INFURIATINGL[Y] OPTIMISTIC LOOK ON YOUR FACE...

...WON'T HURT *YOU PEOPLE* AS MUCH AS THIS WILL.

KILLING THOSE MILLION PEOPLE YOU DON'T EVEN KNOW...

FINE, NII-SAN. I SEE HOW IT IS.

!

...IS WHAT I HATE MOST OF ALL!

WHAT...?

I'M NOT GONNA LET HER STUPID EVIL PLANS BEAT ME.

YOU JUST SIT TIGHT AND WATCH.

I'M FALLING IN LOVE WITH YOU ALL OVER AGAIN.

YOU REALLY ARE AN AWESOME PERSON.

HOW CAN YOU SAY—

WHA... T-T-T-T-TŌ...

WHA—

TŌ—

HA-WHA?

GASP!!

SMIRK...!!

KIRIË.

SHUDDER!!

OH, NO!!

THIS IS NOTHING. I WOULDN'T MAKE YOU USE YOUR POWER TWICE FOR THIS.

DON'T SELL ME SO SHORT, KIRIË SAKURAME.

IT'S NOT SO WEIRD TO WISH FOR THAT.

...OR AT LEAST NOT VERY MANY.

THERE ARE A LOT OF KIDS LIKE YOU, WHO COULDN'T BE YOU.

AND I WANT TO MAKE THIS WORLD A PLACE WHERE THERE AREN'T ANY...

THEN YOU'RE OKAY NOW.

YOU CAN TRUST ME.

I WON'T BETRAY YOU.

...

SHH!

AND I CAN DO IT AGAIN, EASY PEASY.

I'VE BEEN ALONE UP UNTIL NOW.

...WILL FIND EACH OTHER AGAIN.

BESIDES, I'M SURE THAT INCOMPETENT AND I...

I LOVE YOU, KIRIË.

?!

PAT PAT

PFFT

DON'T WORRY, TŌTA. REJECTION IS WHAT HELPS MEN GROW.

WOULD YOU JUST. SHUT. UP! KIRIË SAKURAME.

IT'S NO BIG DEAL.

SHOONK

HRNGH!

GRMK?!

KIRIË!

SO...GO AHEAD... AND TRY. ISN'T THAT... WHAT I'VE BEEN SAYING?

BUT THERE'S NO WAY IT CAN BE POSSIBLE WITHOUT ANY RISK INVOLVED.

I KNOW IT'S DIFFICULT TO GUESS WHAT WILL ACTIVATE A UNIQUE SKILL.

...IT'S A BLUFF.

!

...OKAY. MAYBE I WILL.

I CAN HANDLE GOING BACK THAT FAR. IT'S NOTHING.

IT'S OKAY...

I CAN SEE THE FEAR IN YOUR EYES, KIRIË SAKURAME.

....!

...!

THAT'S ALL I CAN SAY.

THE CHOICE IS UP TO YOU.

SAVING THEM COMES FIRST, NO MATTER WHAT WE HAVE TO DO TO ACCOMPLISH IT!

YOUR PERSONAL EMOTIONS AND MEMORIES ARE NOTHING COMPARED TO THE LIVES OF A MILLION, OR EVEN A THOUSAND PEOPLE!

EXCUSE ME, TŌTA! WHY DO YOU EVEN HAVE TO THINK ABOUT THIS?

THE EXPERIENCES KIRIÉ-CHAN SHARED WITH YOU OVER THE LAST FEW MONTHS ARE IRREPLACEABLE!

AND SHE... SHE'S PREPARED TO GIVE THEM ALL UP TO...

TŌTA-KUN!!

THIS ISN'T A MATTER OF COMPARISON! WE SHOULDN'T COMPARE THESE THINGS!!

HOW CAN YOU SAY THAT, KARIN-SEMPAI?!

UH... GUYS?

NO, KARIN-SEMPAI, ARE YOU SERIOUS?!

EXCUSE ME, KURŌMARU! ARE YOU INSANE?!

SHE'S PLANNING TO REPEAT MORE THAN TEN YEARS OF HER LIFE TO MAKE IT BACK TO THIS POINT IN TIME.

YES...

...

THAT MEANS...

TŌTA.

WH...

WHY ARE YOU BRINGING THAT UP NOW?

YOU KNOW HOW KIRIË FEELS ABOUT YOU, RIGHT?

THERE'S NO TELLING IF SHE'LL BE ABLE TO BUILD THE SAME RELATIONSHIP WITH YOU IN HER NEXT LIFE.

IF SHE GOES BACK IN TIME, EVERYTHING SHE EXPERIENCED WITH YOU WILL HAVE NEVER HAPPENED.

PEOPLE'S HEARTS ARE UNCERTAIN, AND PRONE TO CHANGE.

AND THAT GOES FOR HAPHAZARD, IRRESPONSIBLE BRATS LIKE YOU, TOO.

...AND TO YOU.

TO HER...

THESE LAST FEW DAYS... NO, THESE LAST FEW MONTHS. WHAT DID THEY MEAN?

YUKI-HIME?

TŌTA!

TŌTA!

...

I KNOW YOU CAN'T REALLY USE APPS,

BE QUIET AND LISTEN.

!

SO I OPENED A PRIVATE TELEPATHY CHANNEL THROUGH KARIN.

BUT...

KIRIË IS TELLING THE TRUTH.

NOT EVEN SHE KNOWS HOW FAR BACK IN TIME SHE'LL GO.

IF SHE DIES AND GOES BACK WITHOUT A SAVE POINT,

...!

SHE'LL GO BACK TO WHEN HER POWER FIRST ACTIVATED.

MOST LIKELY...

HRGH ...

KIRIË!!

GO AHEAD... KILL ME.

TIME WILL TURN BACK, AND YOUR WHOLE PLAN WILL GO UP IN SMOKE.

...!

IDIOT KID SISTER! SORRY TO RUIN YOUR FUN!

WHAT DO YOU KNOW ABOUT ME?

NO...

THAT CAN'T BE RIGHT! ACCORDING TO THE REPORT—

DON'T WORRY! JUST DO EVERY-THING YOU CAN!

SO EVERY-ONE! TŌTA!

IF IT STILL DOESN'T WORK, THE INVINCIBLE KIRIË-CHAN WILL USE HER POWERS TO GO BACK AND FIX IT!

YOU LITTLE...!

KIRIË...!

...

...WHAT?

STUPID INCOMPE-TENT.

WHAT ARE YOU CACKLING ABOUT?

I SHOULD HAVE EXPECTED AN INCOMPETENT KID SISTER.

WELL, WITH AN INCOMPETENT BIG BROTHER,

BUT THAT'S JUST A SUPPORT RITUAL.

WE CAN'T GO BACK AND FIX THINGS ANYMORE.

YOU THINK THAT JUST BECAUSE YOU DESTROYED MY SAVE POINT,

THEY'RE NOTHING BUT A PSYCHOLOGICAL TRICK TO TAKE ME BACK TO AN EXACT TIME.

IT'S TRUE.

IMPOSS-IBLE...

I DON'T NEED ONE OF THOSE TO GO BACK IN TIME.

YOU'LL NEVER RECOVER FROM THAT!

YOU'LL NEVER TAKE ANOTHER STEP FORWARD!

HA HA HA HA HA! THAT'LL WORK!

AND YOU CAN WATCH THEM DO IT, WHILE YOU SIT THERE TWIDDLING YOUR THUMBS LIKE AN IDIOT!

I LIKE IT!

THAT'S GOOD ENOUGH FOR ME!! HA HA... HA HA HA!

HA HA HA HA!

YOUR LIFE WILL BE AS GOOD AS OVER!!

HEH.

HA HA HA!
HA HA HA
HA HA
HAH HA

OR WILL YOU KILL A THOUSAND PEOPLE WITH YOUR OWN HANDS?!

YOU NEED TO MAKE UP YOUR MIND!!

WILL YOU JUST SIT THERE AND WATCH, WHILE A MILLION PEOPLE DIE?!

WELL, NII-SAN?!

S.E.P.C

HNGH...

UNLIKE YOU, I'M SURE WE CAN COUNT ON ONE OF THEM TO SACRIFICE THE THOUSAND FOR THE MILLION.

...

...OR THE FOUR-EYES UP THERE MAKE THE DECISION FOR YOU.

YOU COULD HAVE THE PHONY VAMPIRE DOWN HERE...

NO... WAIT...

YOU DON'T HAVE TO CHOOSE.

SHE'S TAKEN KIRIÉ HOSTAGE.

YEAH. RIGHT IN FRONT OF ME.

YOU SEE HER, RIGHT?

...YUKI-HIME.

IT WON'T IMPROVE THE SITUATION FOR YOU.

YEAH, PROBABLY NOT.

BUT IT DOESN'T MATTER WHAT I DO TO HER RIGHT NOW.

GRR ...!

WHICH MEANS... WE HAVE TO FIGURE THIS OUT ON OUR OWN.

I WOULDN'T LET YOU WEASEL YOUR WAY OUT OF IT THAT EASILY!!

I PUT THIS PLAN TOGETHER PIECE BY TINY PIECE!

THE HELL THERE IS! YOU'RE SO STUPID, KUROMARU!!

WHAT?

SOME WAY... TO SAVE THE MILLION PEOPLE ON THE GROUND WITHOUT KILLING THE THOUSAND PEOPLE ON THE TRAIN...

THERE MUST BE SOMETHING...

I *LIKE* THAT FACE, NII-SAN!

HA HA HA HA HA HA HA!

HA.

YOU'RE NOT MAKING ANY SENSE!!

IF I'M THE ONE YOU WANT, WHY DON'T YOU COME AND GET *ME*?!

MY ONLY CHOICE IS TO CRUSH YOU PSYCHOLOGICALLY.

YOU'RE IMMORTAL. IF I WANT TO INFLICT ANY LASTING DAMAGE,

DON'T BE STUPID, NII-SAN.

BUT YOU HAD TO PLAY THE HERO, STICK YOUR NOSE WHERE IT DIDN'T BELONG, AND FALL INTO MY TRAP, JUST LIKE I KNEW YOU WOULD.

WHY SHOULD YOU CARE ABOUT THOSE HUMANS? YOU DON'T KNOW THEM.

YOU REALLY ARE STUPID, NII-SAN.

YOU...

I WANTED TO SEE THE LOOK ON YOUR FACE.

DAMMIT, CUTLASS!!

JUST SO YOU COULD ...?!

D...

THE ARM I CUT OFF?! NO, I THOUGHT I DESTROYED THAT!

IMPOSSIBLE! HOW DID YOU GET OUT OF SOLITARY CONFINEMENT ?!

!

HNGH...

YOU'RE JUST GOING TO HAVE TO BE A LITTLE MORE PARANOID IF YOU WANT TO STOP PEOPLE LIKE US.

THE ARM YOU DESTROYED WAS A FAKE.

YOU DIDN'T MAKE ANY MISTAKES, FOUR-EYES.

AND YOU FELL FOR IT HOOK, LINE, AND SINKER, UQ HOLDER... OR SHOULD I SAY, NII-SAN.

I FED YOU THE INFORMATION ABOUT THE TERRORIST ATTACK TO GET YOU MOVING.

WHY ARE YOU DOING THIS?

CUTLASS, YOU...

TO BE HONEST... I THINK IT'S GONNA BE TOUGH TO SAVE EVERYBODY THIS TIME.

GRR...

350m

EVEN IF I DID SWITCH-EROO THE BOMB, WE'D STILL BE AT GROUND ZERO.

IT WOULDN'T HELP. THE FARTHEST MY POWER CAN SEND SOMETHING IS 350 METERS.

...

...

...IT'S YOUR CHOICE.

...BUT.

THAT VOICE ...!

?!

NII-SAN.

YOU MUST CHOOSE.

NII-SAN.

WELL, THE OBVIOUS SOLUTION...

UH... ER.

WE'RE HERE, BUT WHAT DO WE DO NOW, NII-CHAN?!

WHOOSH

SO...

A THOUSAND PEOPLE IS NOTHING COMPARED TO A MILLION.

...IS TO SACRIFICE ALL THE PEOPLE ON THE TRAIN, RIGHT?

URK...

YEAH... HOW DID I KNOW YOU WERE GONNA SAY THAT...

WE CAN'T JUST LET THESE PEOPLE DIE, JINBEI-SAN!!

HMMM...

WHAT IF WE USE YOUR SWITCHEROO TO TOSS THE BOMB OUTSIDE?!

I KNOW!!

THIS SECOND WAVE ATTACK... IS IT POSSIBLE THAT THEY EXPECTED US TO HOP BACK IN TIME TO STOP THE FIRST ATTACK...

BUT *THIS TIME*, WE SUDDENLY FIND ANOTHER BOMB, AND WE'RE FORCED TO TAKE ACTION.

THERE WAS NO SECOND NUCLEAR EXPLOSION LAST TIME, BEFORE KIRIË TURNED BACK THE CLOCK.

KIRIË!!

BAH

GASP!!

WHAT...?

...AND IT'S A TRAP?

I SEE IT!!

ZAM

WHOOSH

BAH

MIDAIR SHUNDŌ!!

WHOOSH

WHO ARE YOU PEOPLE ?!

WH-WHAT THE—?!

AAAHH!

WAAH?!

YUKIHIRO

WHACK

SORRY! IT'S AN EMERGENCY!

ACK, HEY!

BAH

WE HAVE PERMISSION!

TŌTA-KUN!!

KURO-MARU!

THAT WAY!

WHERE'S THE TRAIN TRACK ?!

WE JUST HAVE TO JUMP DOWN!!

SHA ROW

WHAT'S GOING ON?!

AAAH!!

GOING BACK'LL BE MUCH EASIER THAN GETTING HERE WAS.

OKAY!

IT'S BASICALLY THE SAME PROBLEM WE HAD BEFORE.

HEY, YUKIHIME. WHAT ARE WE GONNA DO HERE?

THERE ARE HUNDREDS OF THOUSANDS... NEARLY A MILLION PEOPLE MOVING IN AND OUT AT ANY GIVEN HOUR OF ANY DAY.

THE MEGA-FLOAT ON THE EARTH'S SURFACE IS A COMMERCIAL DISTRIBUTION CENTER.

...WE'LL HAVE TO CHOOSE TO SACRIFICE THE THOUSAND PASSENGERS.

TO SAVE THE MILLION PEOPLE ON THE MEGA-FLOAT...

DOESN'T IT SEEM STRANGE TO YOU?

WAIT A MINUTE, MISTRESS.

THAT WON'T BE ENOUGH TIME TO EVACUATE ONE MILLION PEOPLE.

EVEN IF WE MANAGE TO KEEP THE TRAIN GOING JUST BARELY ABOVE 100 KM AN HOUR, IT WOULD MAKE IT TO EARTH IN THREE HOURS.

WHAT?

I'LL GO AFTER IT!!

YUKIHIME!! THAT TRAIN IS HEADING FOR EARTH RIGHT NOW, RIGHT?!

I'LL GET WORD TO THE ORBITAL ELEVATOR'S MANAGEMENT!

FOR NOW, WE'LL JUST CATCH UP TO IT!!

THE REST OF YOU, TOO! HURRY!

UGH... OKAY, GO!!

AWW, DAMMIT! FINE!

W-WE'RE ON OUR WAY!!

TURN RIGHT UP AHEAD— THAT'LL LEAD TO THE PUBLIC FLOOR!

WHERE'S THE ELE-TRAIN STATION ?!

!

PA-
LING

カシャン
CLANK

BUT IF WE DON'T STOP THE TRAIN...

...IF THE TRAIN'S SPEED DROPS BELOW 100 KM PER HOUR.

WHAT?!

THE BOMB IS ATTACHED TO A DEVICE THAT WILL SET IT OFF...

...A NUCLEAR BOMB...

...WILL DESTROY THE MEGA-FLOAT AT THE TOWER'S BASE!!

BAM

THIS HAS NEVER HAPPENED BEFORE!

NO... HOW?

WHA...

KIRIË! HEY, KIRIË! WHAT HAPPENED?!

KIRIË, WAIT!

...

WHAT...?

YUKIHIME-SAMA!!

WHAT?!

I'VE LOCATED THE SECOND NUCLEAR EXPLOSIVE!!

IT LEFT 30 MINUTES AGO...

IT ISN'T INSIDE THE STATION!!

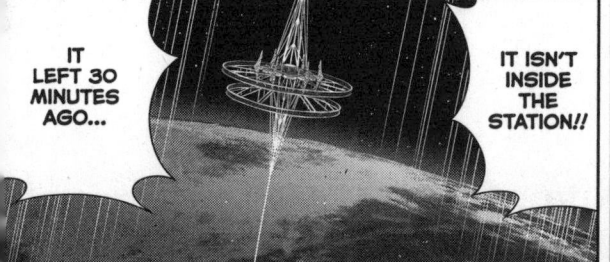

WHERE IS IT?!

STAGE 145: THE MILLION OR THE THOUSAND? OR KIRIË?

CONTENTS

They take down the terrorist, but victory is short-lived...

EXPLOSION IN 00 MIN. 18 SEC.

...as a second wave attack awaits them!

THEY'VE PLANNED A SECOND WAVE ATTACK!!

I FOUND A MEMORY FRAGMENT! THEY WERE PREPARED FOR THEIR MISSION TO FAIL!

WHA-?!

To make matters worse, Kirië's save point has been destroyed, and they can't go back to the past!

MY SAVE POINT...

IT'S BROKEN?

Has UQ HOLDER met their match?!

HEY THERE, NII-SAN.

YOU'RE NOT GONNA KILL ME?

YOU SHOULD.

After beating back Cutlass, UQ HOLDER faces a new threat!

They must go to the Orbital Elevator...

BOOM

...to stop a nuclear explosion!!

仮 UQ HOLDER!

Ken Akamatsu Presents

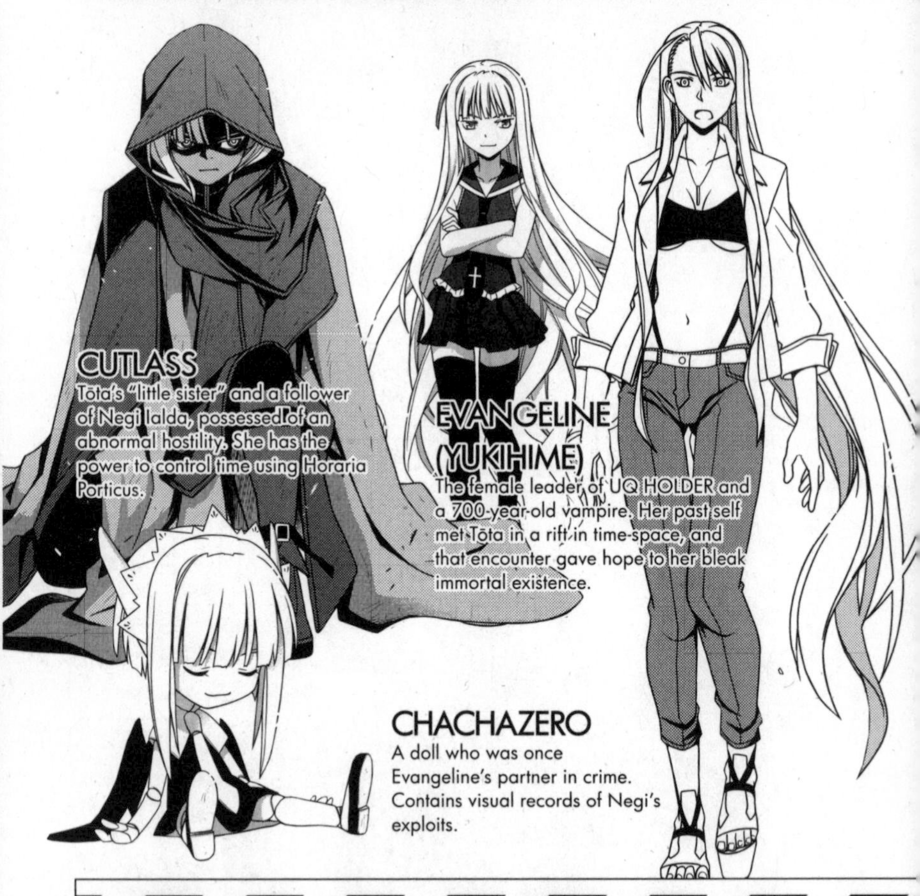

CUTLASS

Tōta's "little sister" and a follower of Negi Ialda, possessed of an abnormal hostility. She has the power to control time using Horaria Porticus.

EVANGELINE (YUKIHIME)

The female leader of UQ HOLDER and a 700-year-old vampire. Her past self met Tōta in a rift in time-space, and that encounter gave hope to her bleak immortal existence.

CHACHAZERO

A doll who was once Evangeline's partner in crime. Contains visual records of Negi's exploits.

KURŌMARU TOKISAKA

UQ HOLDER NO. 11

A skilled fencer of the Shinmei school. A member of the Yata no Karasu tribe of immortal hunters, he will be neither male nor female until his coming of age ceremony at age 16.

KARIN YŪKI

UQ HOLDER NO. 4

Cool-headed and ruthless. Her immortality is S-class. Also known as the Saintess of Steel.

CHARACTERS

TŌTA KONOE

An immortal vampire. Has the ability Magia Erebea, as well the only power that can defeat the Mage of the Beginning, the White of Mars (Magic Cancel) hidden inside him. For Yukihime's sake, he has decided to save both his grandfather Negi and the world.

KIRIË SAKURAME

UQ HOLDER NO. 9

The greatest financial contributor to UQ HOLDER, who constantly calls Tōta incompetent. She can stop time by kissing Tōta.

UQ HOLDER IMMORTAL NUMBERS

JINBEI SHISHIDO

UQ HOLDER NO. 2

UQ HOLDER's oldest member. Became an immortal in the middle ages, when he ate mermaid flesh in the Muromachi Period. Has the "Switcheroo" skill that switches the locations of physical objects.

GENGORŌ MAKABE

UQ HOLDER NO. 6

Manages the business side of UQ HOLDER's hideout and inn. He has a skill known as "Multiple Lives," so when he dies, another Gengorō appears.

UQ HOLDER!

KEN AKAMATSU

vol.17